PRAISE FOR *Finding Soul Rest*

CZ has written a beautiful and timely book. When many are seeking to resume life as normal, he is inviting us to re-examine the depth and possibility of another kind of life, one that brings renewal and hope to the deepest parts of who we are called to be. This book is a real gift.

JON TYSON
author of *Beautiful Resistance* and
lead pastor of Church of the City New York

I know what it's like to live in full-time ministry and service for God and his kingdom only to wake up and realize that my heart was far from God and my soul was battered and tired to the bone! What CZ has gifted to us in *Finding Soul Rest* is a lifeline! He has done some very holy and treasurable legwork here to help lead us in establishing a daily connection with Jesus Christ, our source of rest and life! Whether you just need a place to start or a guide to keep coming back to, this devotional is a powerful resource!

CHRISTY NOCKELS
worship leader, podcaster, and
author of *The Life You Long For: Learning to Live from a Heart of Rest*

From the moment I met CZ, Holy Spirit wisdom and maturity spilled out of him. This devotional, rooted in the Word of God, is no different and is full of practical application that will help you journey toward true rest.

NATALIE GRANT
recording artist, author, and philanthropist

What we don't seem to understand is that finding rest for our souls can be hard work before we come to that place of peace. The way to that place must be sought out and found. CZ explains in this profound book that the way is, in fact, a Person. He knows precisely because he has spent so much of himself seeking and finding and being found by the One who is our peace.

MICHAEL CARD
musician and Bible teacher

# PRAISE FOR *Soul Rest*

As I soak in *Soul Rest*, I'm stirred to examine my bustling mindset and to lean into a kinder rhythm, a Sabbath song. I've put this book on my twice-a-year read list.

PATSY CLAIRMONT
author of *You Are More Than You Know*

I'm grateful for men like Curtis who are making disciples in places that are hard to reach. He is taking a strong stand on the word of God in cities that need it.

FRANCIS CHAN
author of *Crazy Love*

In a 24/7/365 world, we lose sight of the fact that we have been designed to regularly stop and lay everything down. In *Soul Rest*, CZ points the way to finding the true source of life.

TOBYMAC
Grammy award–winning artist, producer, and songwriter

Reading *Soul Rest: Reclaim Your Life. Return to Sabbath* by Curtis Zackery felt like a sweet whisper from God showing me the importance of true rest for my soul. In our busy, rushed, American dream–driven society, *Soul Rest* is an important book every Jesus-follower should read.

MANDISA
contemporary Christian recording artist

*Soul Rest* is a book that helps us to remember and understand how we find our identity and rest in Jesus. This important book helps us understand that our hearts have a longing that can only be satisfied by God.

DR. JOHN M. PERKINS
founder and president emeritus, John & Vera Mae Perkins Foundation

*Soul Rest* is what the church desperately needs. God's rest rescued me from the idols of performance and turned me into a messenger of peace. I never want to go back. May the words on these pages settle deep.

REBEKAH LYONS
author of *You Are Free* and *Freefall to Fly*

Curtis Zackery comes alongside like a spiritual director, pastoring us toward the rest our soul desires. His careful diagnosis of the problem and practical solutions makes *Soul Rest* a must-read for anyone feeling the anxiety in a busy society.

GABE LYONS
president of Q;
author of *Good Faith*, *UnChristian*, and *The Next Christians*

# FINDING SOUL REST

40 DAYS OF
CONNECTING WITH CHRIST

A DEVOTIONAL

CURTIS ZACKERY

KIRKDALE PRESS

*Finding Soul Rest: 40 Days of Connecting with Christ*
A Devotional

Kirkdale Press, 1313 Commercial St., Bellingham, WA 98225
KirkdalePress.com

Print ISBN 9781683594284
Digital ISBN 9781683594291
Library of Congress Control Number 2020943016

Kirkdale Editorial: Abigail Stocker, Deborah Keiser, Matthew Boffey, Jessi Strong
Cover Design: Lydia Dahl
Book Design and Typesetting: Abigail Stocker

The Truth must dazzle gradually
Or every man be blind—

EMILY DICKINSON

# CONTENTS

# INVITATION TO REST

When it comes to learning something new or accomplishing a goal I've set for myself, I have a natural tendency to try to expedite the process. Usually, that includes looking for a book or some resource that will explain in short order what I need to know. That way, I can cut down on the time it will take to endure the process and get to the end much quicker. Maybe you have come to this book with the same hope. Unfortunately, I don't think it will meet your expectations.

To accomplish what the book's title suggests, finding soul rest, we need to know that the only path to do so is found in the subtitle: connecting with Christ. My hope is that this book is an onramp to substantive introspection and time with God, so that he can provide what we really desire.

Some of us reading this are realizing that we have experienced burnout or are simply at the end of our rope. Others of us are reading because we never want to find ourselves in that place. In any case, this book will be most useful to you if you are resolved that it's time to find rest.

My journey toward soul rest began at a convergence of events in my life. My wife and I had been doing good and purposeful work in our neighborhood, but I knew that it wasn't sustainable. Every day, we were helping homeless friends, walking with people in recovery from addiction, and pointing to the hope of Jesus, and yet it felt like something was off. It turned out I was doing a lot of work *for* God, but I wasn't really doing a lot of work *with* God. I was beginning to grow tired, and no vacation or break would suffice. It wasn't a surface kind of tired; it was a soul tired. My identity, worth, and value were found in the things that I was doing for God, and I didn't know how to live from God.

During the same season, my wife and I experienced loss through miscarriage, twice. The second time was further into the pregnancy and was much more physically and emotionally taxing. Experiencing loss, and walking through the pain of grief, only accentuated the disillusionment and frustration that I was feeling in my current condition.

Finally, while all of this was unfolding, I felt terribly alone. Sure, there were incredible people around me who loved me.

But experiencing this time helped me to see that I had never granted anyone permission to enter into the painful places that I was walking through.

We all have our own stories, and the twists and turns look different for each one of us. What I've come to discover is that no matter who we are or where we come from, we cannot maintain health and life the way God intends by our strength alone.

Although something about the term is compelling, you may be asking yourself, what exactly is this "soul rest" that we are hoping to find? I think the answer is most easily summarized by scriptures found in the book of Matthew. In chapter 11, we find Jesus addressing a group of people who have been burdened by the weight of legalistic rules and laws connected to their religion. People are exhausted because they realize that they can never accomplish the righteousness they hope to achieve in their own strength. These people had been living under a teaching that said it was up to them to earn salvation by their ability to do good works. Many were under the belief that those who imposed all of these rules and laws were the ones who could determine whether or not one was good enough to stand underneath the judgment of God. It is in this context that Jesus says the words that must have felt like water in a desert to people who were dry, tired, anxious, and hopeless:

Come to me, all who labor and are heavy laden, and I will give you rest. Take my yoke upon you, and learn from me, for I am gentle and lowly in heart, and you will find *rest for your souls*. For my yoke is easy, and my burden is light. (Matt 11:28–30)

Jesus let them know that he, alone, was the source of hope that they were longing for. He made clear that the teaching of their day was heavy and burdensome. He said that his way was easy and light. Jesus was letting them know that the rest they were longing for didn't just involve taking a break from trying to uphold the rules and laws here on earth. Jesus was letting them know that the rest he wanted them to have was for their souls, and for eternity!

I hope this book serves as a reminder of where true soul rest is found. It is found in the salvation work that could only be accomplished by Jesus on the cross. It is found in the truth that our identity, worth, and value will never be found in what we do but rather in Christ alone. It is found in the reminder that we don't have to carry the heavy baggage connected to our past, which leads to exhaustion. Instead we can turn to Jesus, confess, open our hands, and walk forward, living freely and lightly.

## DAY 1

---

# IN AND DOWN

Search me, O God, and know my heart!
Try me and know my thoughts!
And see if there be any grievous way in me,
and lead me in the way everlasting!

PSALM 139:23-24

Exhausted. Dry. Tired. Disillusioned. Anxious. Stressed. Frustrated. Burned out.

One or a few of these words might describe what you are feeling in life right now. If so, it is important to give yourself permission to ask one big question: why?

It has been said, "The main obstacle to love for God is service for God."[1] It is possible to be working and going so hard *for* God that we forget what it means to be connected *to* God. We must pause from our constant motion to reflect and examine the condition of our soul.

When we discover things in our lives that are out of rhythm with God, our natural tendency is to go "outward and upward" with our response. We go out by confessing our sins, and then offering them up to God himself to forgive, heal, and restore. Instead, it might be time to go "inward and downward"—inward to examine what we feel in our hearts, and downward to discover the roots of where these feelings originate. It is only then that we can bring our true and full self before God and present what truly needs restoration. But, for most of us, this seems a bit scary.

Even though self-evaluation and contemplation are important, fear of what we may find can keep us from doing it. We'd much rather convince ourselves that we have it all together, because this feels like the safer option. But it keeps us from identifying the areas in our lives that need healing, reinforcement, or affirmation. G. K. Chesterton wrote, "If you leave a thing alone, you leave it to a torrent of change. If you leave a white post alone it will soon be a black post. If you particularly want it to be white you must be always painting it again; that is, you must be always having a revolution."[2] Looking inward and asking hard questions can lead to clarity about our condition.

A mistake at this point would be assuming this approach is just a wavering faith in Christ. We seem to think that an internal audit of our spiritual condition is only attributed to angst and disbelief in God. This doesn't have to be the case!

Reflecting and reevaluating can bring encouragement and clarity, which produces rest. A healthy time of prayer and reflection should reinforce the direction and vision the Lord has granted us. Psalm 139 reminds us that inviting God to reveal to us our inner reality leads us to receive clarity of the next right steps in our lives. It is good for us to know where we are so we can understand where we need restoration.

---

What does it look like for you to go "in" and "down" in this season? What do you hope is the outcome?

DAY 2

_____

# TASTE AND SEE

Oh, taste and see that the LORD is good!
Blessed is the man who takes refuge in him!

PSALM 34:8

Those who know me know that I *really* enjoy a good meal. When I taste something good, I let whoever is in my presence know about my satisfaction. There are times when it seems that I can't even contain the audible response, bursting out with an involuntary "mmmm!" at the table. Knowing that many people can relate to this impulse, I can't help but think of the connections to Psalm 34:8. As I taste and see that God is good, my reaction should, similarly, be one that displays my satisfaction.

When I'm served a delicious plate of food, it's not enough for me to just be near the plate of food. Smelling, touching,

4

hearing, or looking at the food won't be enough to know how good it really is. I need to taste it for myself. Many of us haven't felt a deep response to the goodness of God recently because we haven't been tasting for ourselves what it's like to know him. Maybe we've been near God but not connected to God ourselves.

Many of us tend to lean toward stoicism and seriousness when it comes to matters of God. We mainly focus on all the things that are yet to be resolved in our lives, which produces anxiety, stress, and worry. We are so focused on solving problems that we don't take time to celebrate, letting our concerns hold us back from freely worshiping God.

Have you ever been at a wedding or a party when the music starts? The dance floor is empty, and no one seems ready to be the first out there. Then, you see some young children make their way onto the floor, smiling and dancing freely as the band plays. They are not bogged down with the cares of the world, nor consumed with people's opinion of their expression. What a beautiful picture of what it should be like in the heart of our worship. There is freedom in kids' unhindered response.

My friend Keas Keasler once said, "The most theologically appropriate response to the resurrection of Jesus is to dance." Not only do I want to dance physically, but I want my heart to dance in response to the truth and reality of the gospel. Always. I want my instinctive response to the beauty of the gospel to be one that reflects my utter satisfaction. This is a response fueled by gratitude. When my heart is filled with gratitude and my thoughts are filled with thankfulness, it produces rest in my life. Before I focus on what I want and need, I am encouraged and grateful for what I have.

———————————

Reflecting on Psalm 34:8, can you recall a time when you have "tasted and seen," and responded with rejoicing?

---

# THE JOY OF MY SALVATION

Restore to me the joy of your salvation,
and uphold me with a willing spirit.

PSALM 51:12

As soon as the pastor began preaching, I knew he was speaking from a place of deep honesty and vulnerability. He shared a story about how he was looking at some of his old journals and discovered something that was alarming. He noticed that the way that he wrote about his love for God during the early stages of his faith was intimate and urgent. Looking at the heart behind those old words, he knew that, in some ways, his relationship with God had become stale and complacent. This realization led him to ask, "Is it possible that I could have enjoyed Jesus back then more than I do now!?"

Then he challenged us to recall the joy that was present at the beginning of our connection with Jesus. He talked about how criticism and hard days of life and ministry had stolen the smiles and laughter from so many following the Lord. You could just feel the tangible connection of the men and women in the room to the words the speaker was sharing. He noted that, though we often say how thankful we are that we're not the same people we used to be before Christ redeemed our lives, in our actual living it doesn't appear that anything is different as a result of our rescue from death.

I expect that many can relate to this. Maybe there was a time when we were more willing to speak the truth candidly without shying away in fear of judgment or criticism. Maybe we used to dedicate more time to studying the word and prayer than focusing on completing tasks and just being busy. Maybe our faith has become an idea to argue about, rather than a love story with God to share with passion.

Life is filled with twists and turns. Things we experience can shape who we are in hard and purposeful ways. As a result, our view of God and our relationship with him may have been affected in some difficult ways. Although seasons change, God doesn't. Perhaps you now recognize that you need to pray that the Lord would "restore the joy of your salvation." There is joy in his presence. There is peace and rest there. The gospel satisfies, and our work doesn't earn his favor. He is our Salvation.

As you think of Psalm 51:12, can you identify areas where you would like the Lord to restore the joy of your relationship with him?

---

# THE REST IN THE GOSPEL

So then, there remains a Sabbath rest for the people
of God, for whoever has entered God's rest has also
rested from his works as God did from his.

HEBREWS 4:9-10

Have you ever had a key ring that includes a mystery key? You
know the key has to open *something* important, but you're
not quite sure what it is. You look at the key and think to
yourself, "This was important enough to hang on to, so it
must have been significant at some point."

For many of us, this is how we view the gospel. We look
at the story of Jesus' redemption like a key that unlocked
the gate to eternal life and opened up a way to salvation. We
shared a lot about how important this key was when we first
discovered it for ourselves. Over time, the good news of the

gospel is shared less, to the point that it becomes like the key that we know is somehow important to the Christian life, but we can't remember why. We have to remember the significance of the gospel, even as followers of Jesus.

The gospel never ceases to be good news. Yes, the message of the way of Jesus introduces lost and hopeless people to the hope of salvation through Jesus. But we, as followers of Jesus, need to be continually reminded of the truth of this message for ourselves, as it is the very crux of our new life in Christ. The gospel represents the significant and finished work of Christ. Because of his work, we can find rest.

If you were rescued from drowning, it wouldn't take much to convince you to tell the story to others. As a matter of fact, you probably couldn't be kept from sharing it. That's because you'd understand the life-and-death implications of what has happened, and the appreciation for your redeemed life would be more than you could contain. When we remember what we've been rescued from, we will celebrate the Rescuer.

The gospel of Jesus is more than just the moment of conversion; it is also the pathway by which we live. The work on the cross that could only be finished by Christ is indeed just that: finished! No more striving and straining and working to earn our salvation. Remembering that we have been rescued brings rest.

---

## How does the truth of the gospel produce rest in your life today?

---

## DAY 5

---

# TRUE SOUL REST

Yes, my soul, find rest in God;
my hope comes from him.

PSALM 62:5, NIV

When our soul feels worn out and withered, we are tempted to feel defeated. Our natural human impulses aren't always given over to optimism or a glass-half-full mentality. In the midst of any circumstances, it's important to be reminded of where our rest comes from.

There is a famous song that says, "Prone to wander, Lord, I feel it, prone to leave the God I love." Our souls may be seeking solace and satisfaction in a myriad of other things. It is then that we must speak to our own soul to tell it the truth. As it says in Psalm 62, the only source of true and sustainable rest is God.

*The Message* version of Matthew 11:28-30 says, "Are you tired? Worn out? Burned out on religion? Come to me. Get away with me and you'll recover your life. I'll show you how to take a real rest. Walk with me and work with me—watch how I do it. Learn the unforced rhythms of grace. I won't lay anything heavy or ill-fitting on you. Keep company with me and you'll learn to live freely and lightly."

The idea of the "unforced rhythms of grace" brings rest and is a product of a genuine connection with Jesus. We can spend so much time working, striving, straining, and trying to manufacture a connection with God that we forget he desires to provide what we need freely. We are continually burdened by what we are attempting to carry in our own strength. He desires that we would learn to live free and light. There is a real opportunity to find real rest in a real Jesus!

———————————

When you read Matthew 11:28-30,
what speaks to you in this season?

## DAY 6

# IDENTIFYING IDOLS

Therefore, my beloved, flee from idolatry. I speak as
to sensible people; judge for yourselves what I say.

1 CORINTHIANS 10:14-15

There are plenty of potential barriers to intimacy with God. If we are honest, it is easy to identify what keeps us from being fully present with him. John Calvin once wrote, "Every one of us is, even from His mother's womb, expert in inventing idols."³ He later says our hearts are a "perpetual factory of idols." It is not hard to find what holds our affections.

As a matter of fact, we were created by God to worship. In Ecclesiastes 3, and all throughout Scripture, we see that our hearts were designed with an eternal longing for him. The worship we were made for is intended to be given to God alone. Our greatest issue as humans is that we've allowed our affection, intended for God, to instead be directed toward people, things, and ideas. Another word for this is idolatry. When we allow idols to interrupt the connection that God intends for us to have with him, it keeps us from experiencing the fulfillment and satisfaction that only he can provide for us—and robs of him of the worship rightly due him.

Ronald Rolheiser says it best in his book *The Holy Longing*: "It is no easy task to walk this earth and find peace. Inside of us, it would seem, something is at odds with the very rhythm of things and we are forever restless, dissatisfied, frustrated and aching. We are so overcharged with desire that it is hard to come to simple rest."[4] There's nothing wrong with having affections. This is, indeed, the way God created us. We are worshipers by design. Since we all have affections, the question becomes, What do we have affection for?

Paying attention to how we spend our time, our thoughts and our money can help us to identify idols. What we give our lives to shows us our true affections. We can *say* that something is important, but actions speak louder than words. In the same way, our minds go where our affections are. More plainly, we think about the things that are important to us. There's a reason that hundreds of Scriptures talk about money and stewardship. Jesus taught about money more than almost any subject, because he knew how money can hold our hearts. How we spend our money reflects our affections.

When we honestly assess where our hearts are and dare to examine what this means for us, we can identify and address the blockage that has kept us from engaging with God. We need to flee from the idols that have interrupted our true worship.

———————

What are some people, things, or ideas that have created a barrier to intimacy with Jesus?

DAY 7

_____

# A LIGHTER LOAD

This is what the Sovereign LORD, the Holy One
of Israel, says: "In repentance and rest is your
salvation, in quietness and trust is your strength,
but you would have none of it."

ISAIAH 30:15, NIV

In our search for soul rest, we have to begin by laying down
our heavy loads. We all know that it is easier to walk when
you don't have to carry unnecessary weight. This is the epit-
ome of common sense. And yet, when it comes to trying to
move toward freedom and a lightness in our lives, we hold
onto the heavy weight of sins and old patterns.

Think of Bible stories that paint the picture of the kind
of repentance God intends for his people. There is a stopping, a 180-degree turn from the direction leading away from
God, and a returning to the one that can provide restoration.

Consider the parable of the prodigal son (Luke 15). He had a moment of awareness (stopped), realized that his current way of life was not working (turned around), and traveled back home (returned).

The son's woes began when he tried to secure fulfillment apart from his father. Similarly, we usually come up with our own strategy to remedy our situation according to our own ideas, strength, and abilities. And yet, just like in that story, it is only the Father who can provide the restoration we desire. Our job is to let go and repent of what we've chosen for satisfaction and return to God. Only he can provide restoration. We return, but he does the work.

In Isaiah 30:15, the prophet makes it clear to the people what path leads to true rest. He points out that even though they know this, they have chosen their own way ("but you would have none of it"). In the case of that story, they chose military strength to be their salvation, rather than the salvation that comes from God. If we are honest, we can relate. We know that God alone satisfies, but we often simply refuse to go to him. Instead, we trust in our own ability to contend for ourselves.

As we desire to find rest and connect to Christ, we will identify things that we use as our practical salvation instead of God. Frankly, we need to repent of them. We need to rest in the salvation that God brings. We need to quiet our impulses and trust in Christ and his finished work on the cross.

Are there things or ideas that you need to repent of?
What does it look like for you to return to God and be received?

DAY 8

---

# FEEL YOUR FEELINGS

Trust in the Lord with all your heart, and
do not lean on your own understanding.
In all your ways acknowledge him, and
he will make straight your paths.

PROVERBS 3:5-6

When our first son Noah started having screen time, we wanted to find shows for him to watch that would be edifying and safe. One of the shows we found was *Daniel Tiger's Neighborhood*. It's a modern iteration of a program I loved as a child, *Mr. Rogers' Neighborhood*. Both shows focus on establishing good values and self-awareness for children. While watching *Daniel Tiger's Neighborhood*, I think I may have learned more than Noah. In one of the episodes, the main lesson was that it was good to allow yourself to experience and feel your emotions. The characters sang a song that goes, "It's okay to feel sad, sometimes. Little, by little, you'll feel better again." The simplicity of the song helped me see that what I wanted for both my son and myself was the permission to feel.

It has been said, "In neglecting our intense emotions, we are false to ourselves and lose a wonderful opportunity to know God. We forget that change comes through brutal honesty and vulnerability before God."[5] For a long time, I would tell myself that feelings were bad and that I needed to suppress them in order to be a good Christian person. I've since learned that acknowledging and feeling my emotions helps me to have the wherewithal to be clear about the areas I need Christ to redeem and restore, so that I can find rest. Emotions aren't a bad thing; rather, it is important to be emotionally healthy.

In order to trust in the Lord with all of your heart, you need to give him *all* of your heart. Sometimes we have a tendency to explain away certain emotions and feelings, believing they have no place before God. We need to be aware of and healthy in our emotions. God wants all of us, and we need to trust that he is big enough to redeem and restore the places that need healing and wholeness in our lives.

---

What parts of your heart, or feelings you have,
do you withhold from God?

---

---

# DEVOUR THE WORD

Blessed is the man who walks not in the counsel of
the wicked, nor stands in the way of sinners, nor sits
in the seat of scoffers; but his delight is in the law of
the LORD, and on his law he meditates day and night.

PSALM 1:1-2

The Bible says to love the Lord your God with all your
mind, and I think meditation is the key to actively doing so.
Christian meditation is based upon on listening and consid-
eration and, ultimately, leads to a connection to the rest-filled
reality of the gospel.

Many followers of Jesus may be a bit leery of the idea of
meditation because of its connections to various other reli-
gious practices. However, meditation is a thoroughly biblical
and deeply spiritual practice. Meditation was very familiar
to the authors of Scripture, and the word or idea appears in

the Bible fifty-eight times. Genesis 24:63; Psalm 63:6; 119:97, 148; and, of course, Psalm 1:2, are just a few familiar instances where meditation is mentioned. Some Christians may believe that mediation is an ineffective use of time, but I think the scriptural examples show us that there is a vital need to develop this practice.

That said, there are some important distinctions to note when seeking to grow in the practice of meditation. Some meditation is, at its core, an attempt to empty the mind. Christian meditation is a practice for filling the mind—with God's truth. Some approach meditation with the hopes of detaching from the world and becoming free from its burdens in hopes of experiencing nirvana; there is no deity to whom you attach. The Christian method says we need to gain understanding so we can rightly engage with the world, which leads to a richer attachment to God, the fear of whom is the beginning of wisdom.

When I was in Israel, I learned to use the Hebrew word *haga* to describe meditation on Scripture. The type of meditation I was learning about could not be explained as a mere memorization tactic. To *haga* was to devour the word, like a pride of lions circling and eating its prey. The idea is to move the word from outside of us to inside of us.

During that same trip, we briefly observed a class filled with students of the Bible. It was explained that they would spend eight to ten hours a day in the scriptural text. In just the few moments that I witnessed this group, I was moved to tears. The way they clearly engaged the text with all of their heart, mind, soul, and strength was deeply compelling. The emotion and anticipation in the reading felt electric in the room. They longed to not just know the words but understand them deep in their souls. This, I believe, is God's desire for Christian meditation. This is his desire for us, his children.

––––––––––––––

What does meditation look like in your life?

---

# A NOISY GONG

If I speak in the tongues of men and of angels,
but have not love, I am a noisy gong
or a clanging cymbal.

1 CORINTHIANS 13:1

Most people associate 1 Corinthians 13 with Valentine's Day, weddings, and greeting cards. Although there is a beautiful and poetic quality in the language and writing, there is nothing sentimental about it. The chapter offers a direct and important challenge, if we are open to receiving it.

In the Bible, the Corinthians were enamored with people who used fancy and eloquent speech. Paul knew this and issued a direct reminder to the readers of the letter. "If I speak in the tongues of men and of angels, but have not love, I am a noisy gong or a clanging cymbal" (1 Cor 13:1). He's lightly using hyperbole here to cover *any* means of communication, while directly addressing the specific areas that he's talked about in the letter. It doesn't matter how beautiful it sounds or how compelling the delivery, without love the fancy communication means nothing.

I don't want to be a noisy gong. A noisy gong or a clanging cymbal startles you and causes you to pause. But just making a loud noise usually isn't very purposeful, in and of itself. Without love as the driving force, our communication can create the same effect. It may cause people to pause for a second and garner people's attention, but without love there is nothing of substance attached. This fact led me to consider my motivations when I talk about Jesus, as well.

In Matthew 6:1, Jesus says, "Beware of practicing your righteousness before other people to be seen by them, for then you will have no reward from your Father who is in heaven." If we aren't careful, it can be more important to us that people think we are good than that *he* is good. There is an important question that I ask myself to help to determine my motives from time to time: "Am I doing this *so that* God loves me or *because* God loves me?" I must evaluate if my actions are based on an effort to earn God's love or come as the result of his love for me.

It's scary how easily we can slip into noisy gong mode. For example, we can do nice things for others and then find passive ways to let them know what we did. We can say things on social media that are directed toward one person, but we really want *everyone* to see what we said and how we said it to that one person. We can share a hope-filled message about Jesus but have a secret desire to be celebrated for the delivery and not care if it leads the listener to heart-change.

I used "we," but I certainly know that I've been guilty of all of those things at times. First Samuel 16:7 says, "For the LORD sees not as man sees: man looks on the outward appearance, but the LORD looks on the heart."

I don't want to be a noisy gong. If I am, I'm only left to be assessed by my abilities rather than pointing to Christ and resting in him.

_____

As you look inward, are there areas of your service to him that have been tainted by selfish motivation?

---

# ROOTED

Therefore, as you received Christ Jesus the Lord,
so walk in him, rooted and built up in him and
established in the faith, just as you were taught,
abounding in thanksgiving.

COLOSSIANS 2:6-7

In the Bible, trees are often used as metaphors to describe what our connection to Christ can and should be like. When I think of trees, two main ideas come to mind, both involving its roots.

First, roots are vital to the tree receiving the nutrients it needs to grow. When the tree is properly rooted, the tree produces life.

Let's take an orange tree, for example. You can't walk up to an orange tree and tell it to make you an orange. An orange tree cannot produce fruit on command. But, if a tree is properly rooted and planted, it will produce good fruit naturally, as a result of the life-giving elements that come through its roots. We, too, need to be properly rooted in Christ. As we are rooted, we will make good fruit naturally as a result of our connection to him.

When we produce our own fruit in our own efforts, it is not real, substantive fruit. It's more like plastic, or fake fruit. I remember as a child seeing a realistic, delicious-looking piece of fruit and attempting to take a huge bite out of it, only to discover that it was hollow inside. It had the appearance of healthy and delicious fruit, but it had no real substance. When you think about the fruit that comes from your life, is it produced by your work or God's work? Drinking deeply of Jesus and the truth of his gospel as we are led by the Spirit produces real, substantial, and sustainable fruit.

Second, roots also help trees remain properly planted. Storm winds and rains can come, but when a tree is properly rooted, it will keep standing. Think about palm trees that endure hurricane winds in south Florida. It's amazing to see them in the background of news reports when a storm is occurring. Sometimes they lean so far back they're almost parallel to the ground. After the storm, you can find bark and leaves from the palm trees scattered all over the streets, but the tree still stands tall, because it is properly rooted. The gospel gives us proper roots that help us remain steadfast in the midst of all types of situations.

When we are rooted in Christ, we can rest knowing that he will supply everything we need for our lives and help us remain immovable in the midst of whatever life throws at us.

———————

When you think about being rooted in Christ, what does that look like in your life?

---

# BE STILL AND KNOW

Be still, and know that I am God.

PSALM 46:10

There are so many things that are inherent to today's culture that keep us from giving ourselves permission to take care of ourselves and do the hard work of introspection. One of the biggest ones is what many people call FOMO, or fear of missing out. This fear can be one of the reasons we feel hesitant to pull back and step out of our normal rhythm. We need to let go of the idea that always *doing* something is the only way to experience life. There is a "life that is truly life" that we can only experience when we stop and commune with the Spirit (1 Tim 6:19 NIV). We must combat the dominant forces of busyness and noise in our culture.

When I finally gave myself permission to pay attention to inner work, I initially made a mistake. I approached the spiritual work as a box to be checked off a list. I wanted to hurry up and get through it so I could get back in the game and do the things that I was supposed to do. I wanted to find soul rest, but it was with the motivation to be a better, stronger Christian—solely to get back to work. I was missing the point. God was asking me if it was enough to just be with him, and I quickly reverted to my desire to do the things that I was doing "for" God.

When our souls are in a disturbed state, it's easy to confuse what we are doing *for* God and what we are doing *from* God. We truly want what has become a duty to be a delight, but we cannot reach this point if we are not willing to simply sit at the feet of Jesus. A well-known story about Mary and Martha comes to mind. Mary thought it was enough to be with Jesus, in his presence and listening to his teaching. It's easy to automatically shift to the thinking Martha had, which was to be busy working, as if that is more spiritual. But Jesus himself is always the point. We can be working for Jesus and forget that anything good, true, and sustainable comes from Jesus.

One of the most famous Bible verses is Psalm 46:10: "Be still, and know that I am God." Our perpetual motion will not allow us the opportunity to recognize the breadth of God's provision and protection. We have to stop moving to be still. This thought is not a revolutionary insight, but it took me a while to figure it out for myself. Our movement and constant "doing" prevents us from fully knowing the love of God.

———————————————

What does it look like for you to be still
and know that God is God?

———————————————

---

# NO MATTER WHAT

Do not be anxious about anything, but in everything
by prayer and supplication with thanksgiving
let your requests be made known to God.

PHILIPPIANS 4:6

When we are feeling anxious and in a state of unrest, we tend to think that it's up to us to figure our way out of our condition. But in the book of Philippians, Paul reminds us that there is a strategy to access God's strength to combat anxiety and uncertainty.

First, be calm: "Rejoice in the Lord always; again I will say, rejoice. Let your reasonableness be known to everyone. The Lord is at hand; do not be anxious about anything, but in everything by prayer and supplication with thanksgiving let your requests be made known to God. And the peace of God, which surpasses all understanding, will guard your hearts and your minds in Christ Jesus" (Phil 4:4–7). Paul reminds us here to rejoice regardless of our current situation. But when our anxieties do rise, we bring them to the Lord and trust that we have presented them to the only one who has the power to hear us and do something about it. We need to replace our anxieties with expectant prayer. Once we've offered our requests to him, we can find peace because of our assuredness in who he is.

Second, be connected: "Finally, brothers, whatever is true, whatever is honorable, whatever is just, whatever is pure, whatever is lovely, whatever is commendable, if there is any excellence, if there is anything worthy of praise, think about these things. What you have learned and received and heard and seen in me—practice these things, and the God of peace will be with you" (Phil 4:8–9). It's easy for us to focus on the hard things in our lives and be distracted from the goodness of who God is. We are tempted, at times, to continue to dwell on our issues even after we've offered them to Jesus. Paul reminds us to instead turn our attention to this list of beautiful things that are true about God so that we aren't completely consumed with our circumstances. We find peace and rest as we wait for the Spirit to move.

Third, be courageous: "I have learned in whatever situation I am to be content. I know how to be brought low, and I know how to abound. In any and every circumstance, I have learned the secret of facing plenty and hunger, abundance and need. I can do all things through him who strengthens me" (Phil 4:11b-13). Because of the greatness of the one to whom we pray, our confidence amid our circumstances can remain constant. Paul lays out some clear examples of how he has had highs and lows but has remained faithful to the truth, sustained through all of it because of the power of the Lord. Knowing that God is with us in both hard and good times reminds us of his abiding love.

———————

Do you have a hard time trusting God no matter what? What are some ways you can grow in this?

---

# THE ORIGINAL,
# SHIMMERING SELF

Nothing is covered up that will not be revealed, or
hidden that will not be known. Therefore whatever
you have said in the dark shall be heard in the light,
and what you have whispered in private rooms
shall be proclaimed on the housetops.

LUKE 12:2-3

We all value and long for authenticity and vulnerability. We
often ask or even demand it from others, yet we may not
understand what it means for us to live it out in our own
lives. I think it is partly difficult because we are terrified
of what we might find if we examined the recesses of our
hearts. It's time that we grant ourselves the permission to
look inward.

Our culture often celebrates any voluntary work that we do on our outside self. Losing weight, working out, and changing our hair or wardrobes are things we esteem regardless of the investment necessary to pull it off. But when we start talking about counseling or doing inner work, the stigma attached can have a lot of negativity connected to it. It keeps us from sharing about it, let alone pursuing holistic health. Even in church, a place that is supposed to be known for vulnerability, we usually look down upon those that take us up on offers to be real.

Frederick Buechner says in his work *Telling Secrets*, "The original, shimmering self gets buried so deep that most of us end up hardly living out of it at all. Instead, we live out all the other selves, which we are constantly putting on and taking off like coats and hats against the world's weather."[6] This quote rings all too true for so many people. Not only is it difficult to live as your true self, but it's even harder to know who your true self is. There have been so many masks, defenses, and pretenses that we have piled on top of one another that we don't know where our true selves begin and end. Because of the stigma attached to inner work, we would rather put forward a "representative," rather than the authentic individual that we are.

The thought that we could finally remove all the layers and masks and get to the heart of who we truly are is exciting and liberating. The issue is, if we allow our true self to come forward, we have no idea what we will find. And, once we make the discovery, we don't know if anyone will want to accept us. God already knows what is in our hearts; there is nothing we can withhold from him. We need God's help to reveal the ways we have been keeping our true self from coming forward. Then, we need to trust his gentle and kind love to restore our hearts.

———————————

What hats and coats do you put on
against the world's weather?

DAY 15

---

# HIS WAYS ARE HIGHER

For my thoughts are not your thoughts, neither are
your ways my ways, declares the LORD. For as the
heavens are higher than the earth, so are my ways
higher than your ways and my thoughts
than your thoughts.

ISAIAH 55:8-9

In Mark 2, the word was spreading that Jesus was making his way back home. Everyone was talking about the messages and miracles of Jesus and wanted to see them for themselves. A paralytic man and his friends also heard Jesus was coming, and they set out to see him in hopes that they could experience his healing powers firsthand. The story goes like this:

Many were gathered together, so that there was no more room, not even at the door. And he was preaching the word to them. And they came, bringing to him a paralytic carried by four men. And when they could not get near him because of the crowd, they removed the roof above him, and when they had made an opening, they let down the bed on which the paralytic lay. And when Jesus saw their faith, he said to the paralytic, "Son, your sins are forgiven." (Mark 2:2–5)

As amazing as it is to hear that your sins are forgiven, I have to imagine that, at first, Jesus' response baffled them. I would assume that, like me, these men were expecting Jesus to tell their friend to get up and walk. They probably had an expectation that he would heal their friend physically. In fact, everyone there was looking to witness something spectacular. Jesus, on the other hand, understood the most significant and meaningful form of healing this man needed. One of the great lessons that we can take away from his immediate response is that Jesus is focused most on the condition of this man's soul. It is all within his power to heal either the inside or the outside, but Jesus knew what this man's healing should look like.

It is up to us to bring our condition to him and submit to his will and leadership in our lives. Isaiah 55:8–9 says, "For my thoughts are not your thoughts, neither are your ways my ways, declares the LORD." Sometimes we feel disappointed when it seems like we aren't getting the answer to prayer that we hope for. It's important for us to consider that maybe it's because God knows better than we do what we need.

———————————

Have you found yourself disappointed in
what seemed like an unanswered prayer,
only to realize that God knew what you needed?
How can you grow in the prayer "Your will be done"?

## DAY 16

---

# WHERE'S MY HELP?

I lift up my eyes to the hills.
From where does my help come?
My help comes from the LORD,
who made heaven and earth.

PSALM 121:1-2

It's good to know what to do when something goes wrong. We know that fire drills, escape routes, and the like are important procedures for children to practice. We want to make sure that no matter what happens, they will be prepared to respond and move toward a place of safety. We overcommunicate these steps and procedures because we want to make sure that in a moment of crisis and in times of distress, they will go to the proper source for help.

When I was growing up, parents, teachers, and school administrators taught us about an initiative called the

Helping Hands Safety Program. If a child happened to be walking through a neighborhood and felt scared, lost, or in danger, they could look for the printed "Helping Hands" sign in the window of a home or a business. This marker immediately provided assurance that it was a safe place and help could be found there. That clarity of direction was important because if there was ever someone who wanted to do you harm, they would most likely try to distract you with things that seem tempting and make you lose focus on where you could find real help.

In our adult lives, we still often find ourselves in situations that require help. Too often, we turn to *our* abilities, *our* ingenuity, *our* effort, *our* righteousness, *our* religion, and *our* way for help first. When we are searching for a source of peace, direction, and rest, we forget the emergency procedures. We know where to look and where help is found, but we get distracted. Psalm 121:1–2 reminds us when it says, "I lift up my eyes to the hills. From where does my help come? My help comes from the Lord, who made heaven and earth."

As we seek to grow and be shaped in this new season, our temptation is to try to figure things out with our ingenuity and ideas leading the way. Sometimes we think if we just lend our best thinking to a problem, we will be able to take care of it ourselves. We need to continually remind ourselves and each other where to go when we are in distress. The Lord wants us to know that he is the source of our help, and he can certainly handle the responsibility. Just as the verse reminds us, he "made heaven and earth."

---

What is an area in your life in which you've been looking for help from sources other than God?

# A MASTERPIECE

He has made everything beautiful in its time.
Also, he has put eternity into man's heart, yet so that
he cannot find out what God has done from
the beginning to the end.

ECCLESIASTES 3:11

Have you ever read the book of Ecclesiastes? On the surface, all it seems to be is a commentary on the brokenness of humanity and our limitations within the bounds of the short amount of time we have here on earth. Sounds kind of burdensome and depressing, right?

Indeed, the intention of the writer is that we would feel the hopelessness that comes from following our own pursuits and attempting to fulfill our deepest longings with things and ideas that are simply not meant to satisfy us. We live on a linear timeline. We are born, and then we die. The length of that experience obviously varies for everyone, but it ends the same way, nonetheless.

However, it is not the intention of the author that we remain in a state of despair. He writes that God "has made everything beautiful in its time. Also, he has put eternity into man's heart, yet so that he cannot find out what God has done from the beginning to the end" (Eccl 3:11). What we see here is some otherworldly good news in the midst of what is a pretty gloomy prognosis for us on earth. God has placed a longing in the hearts of humanity that is acutely aware of the greater, eternal God who exists outside of the bounds of time. He has made everything beautiful within time and, incredibly, has a plan outside of time that is greater and more wonderful than we could ever fathom.

Between the years 1508 and 1512, under Pope Julius II, Michelangelo was commissioned to paint the ceiling of the Sistine Chapel. This piece is considered a masterwork that changed the course of Western art and is widely understood to be one of the most significant artistic accomplishments in history. I think about what it must have been like to walk into the chapel only a matter of months into this project. If you were to look up to the ceiling, all you might have been able to see would be a smattering of various lines, colors, and strokes. You might have been able to see some of the beautiful beginnings of what would ultimately be the result, but you wouldn't know how the whole thing connected together.

But obviously, Michelangelo knew what he was creating, and when we see it today, we see what he intended from the start.

Just like with Michelangelo, if we can fully appreciate the process and see the beauty in what God is doing, our contentment will increase, allowing us to be who God has designed us to be in our current situations. When we can rest in the knowledge that God is at work while we are waiting, we can have peace in our tension-filled lives concerning direction and vision for the future. The Scriptures remind us that "no one can find out what God has done from the beginning to the end," but we can continue to do the next right thing and trust that he is creating a beautiful masterpiece for which only he knows the plans.

———————

How can you grow in your trust that God is working
in ways you cannot see?

---

# RUN/WALK METHOD

He gives power to the faint, and to him who has no
might he increases strength. Even youths shall faint
and be weary, and young men shall fall exhausted;
but they who wait for the LORD shall renew
their strength; they shall mount up with wings
like eagles; they shall run and not be weary;
they shall walk and not faint.

ISAIAH 40:29-31

Running is a hobby that I've grown a great affection for over
time. As I've continued to run, I've learned that there are
many different ways to approach the practice. As I was looking to improve my time leading up to a training period for
a half-marathon, I had a conversation with an avid runner.
He shared with me that one of the ways that marathoners
prepare for a race is with an approach called the run/walk

method. For example, a runner may choose to run for five minutes and walk for one minute, sticking to this rhythm throughout the entirety of the race. To be honest, I immediately scoffed at the idea. I thought, "Stop and walk? That doesn't seem helpful!" Sensing my hesitation, he challenged me to try it out. As you'll probably guess, it was extraordinarily effective.

The challenge with this method is not in the latter stages of the race but at the beginning. It takes great discipline to stop and walk when you still have all of your energy and it feels like you could just keep sprinting. It takes great self-control to stick to the plan, knowing that there is a long race ahead and you'll need that energy to stretch over the long haul. This process is a picture of a sustainable rhythm.

When it comes to our spiritual life, we need the humility to know we can't just push through in our own strength, as well as the discipline to rest. Even when it comes to how we approach studying Scripture, prayer times, fasting, or any spiritual discipline, we need to identify what will sustain these rhythms. It is important, even in the times when it feels like we can keep doing things on our own, to stop, rest, and ask the Spirit of God to give us what we need to run this race of life for his glory until the end.

How do you attempt to sustain your spiritual life
in your own strength?

DAY 19

# UNDER CONTROL

So I do not run aimlessly; I do not box as
one beating the air. But I discipline my body
and keep it under control, lest after preaching
to others I myself should be disqualified.

1 CORINTHIANS 9:26-27

I remember the day my dad taught me how to shoot a basketball correctly. Until that point, I had a method that I had developed over time to get the ball up to the hoop. The form was sloppy, but I figured out how to get the job done. It mainly consisted of me pushing the ball up from my chest and heaving it forward. My dad showed me the benefit of shooting with your elbow in closer to your body and lined up with the front of the hoop.

At first, doing it this way was uncomfortable, because I had my own established rhythm. But slowly, with some practice,

I began to see how this could enhance my ability to play. It was actually working! I stayed there with him shooting for a while and became a bit more comfortable.

After my dad had left the park, though, I immediately started playing a game with some friends. Over the course of the game, all of the helpful knowledge I had just acquired slowly began to wear off, and I went right back to shooting the old way. It was clear that it was going to take some time to establish this new way, and it was going to take practice before it would happen naturally.

Although the rest we are seeking is supernatural in nature, the rhythms of rest take practice. It takes intentionality to develop new spiritual rhythms, and at first it may feel a bit uncomfortable. Living and working from rest is not our default way of thinking, nor is it celebrated by culture, so finding space for rest and incorporating it into our lives can be hard. Just as Paul instructed in Philippians 4:9, we should "practice these things" and trust that God himself will grant us the peace that we need.

---

Do you regularly practice spiritual rhythms?
How can you grow in this area?

---

# PLUGGED IN

I am the vine; you are the branches. Whoever
abides in me and I in him, he it is that bears much
fruit, for apart from me you can do nothing.

JOHN 15:5

If my phone battery was drained, the first thing I would do is connect the charger to my phone and immediately look for an outlet. What if, once I found one, I simply laid the plug-end of the charger on the floor *near* the outlet in the wall? You would quickly explain to me that it is not enough for the charger to be close to the source of power. If I wanted to charge my phone, I would need to actually plug it in.

Often, we are content to be *near* the things of Jesus but not actually connected to him. We find ourselves reading books about the Bible rather than reading the Bible itself. We listen to other people worship rather than sing the authentic song of worship that comes from our hearts. There is so much to learn from the writings, thoughts, and opinions of others when it comes to the Bible and Jesus, but there is nothing like a personal encounter with Christ for ourselves.

In John 15, Jesus gives a picture of what it means to connect with him like this. He says that just like a vine provides the life and nutrients necessary for its branches to produce, so he is our source of life. If those branches are disconnected, they will not have what they need to bear fruit! But if the branches are connected, they rest in the fact that they bear fruit by remaining connected to the vine, not by their own power.

God's desire for us is that we would be fully alive. Our flourishing only comes as a result of our connectedness. It is not up to us to provide the power, but only to tap into it. We find rest when we stop striving and straining to produce and instead channel our energy toward connection. Many of us have been content to be near the Source of life but not actually connected to him. We need the Spirit of God to speak to us and lead and direct our lives.

---

Are there areas in your life in which you recognize you're near but not actually "plugged in" to Christ?

DAY 21

---

# TILLING THE SOIL

Behold, you delight in truth in the inward being,
and you teach me wisdom in the secret heart.
Purge me with hyssop, and I shall be clean;
wash me, and I shall be whiter than snow.

PSALM 51:6-7

While we were still living in Richmond, California, we decided to take on a backyard renovation project. We thought it would be an amazing thing to have a backyard that would allow us to host people, have barbecues, and gather. I'm not the handiest guy, so my wife and I knew that we'd probably be biting off more than we could chew, but that didn't stop us. With the ingenuity of a great friend and the helping hands of some of our church community, we set out to complete the project.

At first glance, our "before" yard seemed perfectly fine—it was green and beautiful. But upon closer inspection, you would realize that the appearance was not reflective of the reality: the yard wasn't grass, it was weeds. The yard had the appearance of health, but there was no real substance there. And, aside from it being a cosmetic issue, the weeds produced small burrs with spiked surfaces that would annoyingly stick to your feet and clothes.

We needed to start from scratch. To do so, the first order of business was to use a rototiller. A rototiller is a big machine with circular blades that dig up the ground, get under the surface, and uproot the weeds. On the first couple of passes, it was almost as if the tiller was bouncing on top of the ground. The soil was so hard that it was terribly difficult to break the surface. Once we were able to get beyond the surface and to really dig up the weeds that had been infesting the yard, we began to run into other issues.

We began finding all types of foreign objects in our way. Old bottles, rocks, trash, and debris were buried everywhere. I had no idea that all of this was under the surface and had been affecting the proper growth of the grass. It's clear that the garbage and debris had been here for a long time and were long overdue for removal. This work slowed down the process but was necessary for an actual fresh start and to prepare the ground for new growth. The garbage was hidden from sight, but it was hampering real growth.

This process is the perfect metaphor for what it means for us to do the inner work of preparing our hearts to encounter the soul rest that comes only from Jesus. Based solely on appearances, we may look like everything is okay, but we need to do the hard work of moving beyond the surface and getting to underlying issues. When we take steps toward gaining clarity and healing in the Lord, it takes patience and intentionality, but on the other side is real growth.

———————————

When was the last time you tilled the soil of your heart?

DAY 22

---

# LEARNING TO LAMENT

How long, O LORD? Will you forget me forever?
How long will you hide your face from me?

PSALM 13:1

All too often, situations in life lead us to ask the question "Why?" And seldom do we feel like we have any good answers. Every day people experience loss or disruption of a dream. When we are in these places of confusion and pain, we often feel the desire to release or escape some of the pressure we're feeling. One reason our response in these situations tends to be unhealthy or even harmful to ourselves or others is because we don't know how to lament.

Lament is a passionate expression of grief or sorrow that helps us to acknowledge our pain and mourn our reality. This type of acknowledgement of our true feelings doesn't readily exist in our culture. Most of us would much rather move on quickly and minimize the hurt. Instead of lamenting, we've developed coping mechanisms that keep us from having to deal with the implications of how we really feel.

The beauty of lament is that it allows us the freedom to lay our utter grief before God and know that he hears us. One of the places that you'd think would be the best for lament is the church. But, because lament is not regularly practiced in many church cultures, many feel alienated and disconnected when they feel like they're unable to bring this part of themselves to the community. We need a space to feel supported to go before the throne of God and open our hearts to him—no matter how messy.

We see examples of lament all throughout the narrative of Scripture. Psalm 13 offers a vivid example. The psalmist honestly and wholeheartedly pours out his feelings before God, and not all of them are uplifting in nature. He expresses his confusion and disillusionment in the midst of his situation. The writer is not exuding hopefulness. In his transparency, he is trusting the Lord to be able to handle his honest words and feels comfortable enough not to hold back. He expresses his despair in his current reality and that God does not seem present in it. Rather than finding resolution in some happy ending, the writer states that God has been good in the past and, for that reason, he will give him the benefit of the doubt. Then the psalm ends. Talk about a beautiful example of lament. He acknowledges the power and goodness of God but honestly states that he sees no immediate hope on the horizon. He's saying, "God, I'm at the end of my rope, and unless you show up, nothing will ever change." It is in this type of process that we can allow the honest space for God to minister to our hearts.

Real lament leads us to rest. When we make room for lament, we voluntarily hit rock bottom, helping us to find the firm footing that accompanies an accurate understanding of our situation. As Christopher J. H. Higgins writes, "It is precisely those who have the closest relationship with God who feel most at liberty to pour out their pain in protest to God—without fear of reproach. Lament is not only *allowed* in the Bible; it is modeled for us in abundance. God seems to want to give us as many words with which to fill out our complaint forms as to write our thank-you notes."[7]

---

Is lament a part of your connection with Christ?
How can you grow in this area?

# DAY 23

---

# LETTING GOD TAKE CARE OF YOU

For I will satisfy the weary soul,
and every languishing soul I will replenish.

JEREMIAH 31:25

Practicing and attempting to grow in our appreciation of the Sabbath helps us to understand a proper view of ourselves in light of who God is. Marva Dawn wrote in *Keeping the Sabbath Wholly*: "A great benefit of Sabbath keeping is that we learn to let God take care of us—not by becoming passive and lazy, but in the freedom of giving up our feeble attempts to be God in our own lives."[8]

At our core, many of us are genuinely tired in ways that we didn't even know were possible. We are exhausted from attempting to govern on our own every aspect of our life.

The practice of honoring the Sabbath and seeking to keep it holy removes the focus from ourselves and focuses on the rescuing and restorative power of God. By default, we are preconditioned to care for ourselves in every way, shape, and fashion. We need to intentionally lay ourselves aside and seek the magnificent Savior for who he really is.

God, our creator, knows us better than we know ourselves. In yielding to his proper position as the Rest Giver, we are submitting to the one who best knows how to care for us. If we attempt to find our own rest, we will always be left wanting. Think about how often people go on vacation only to find themselves more tired than when they left in the first place. If you add parenting children into the mix, this holds especially true!

In Jeremiah 31:25 it says, "For I will satisfy the weary soul, and every languishing soul I will replenish." It's this type of hope that we long to see fulfilled in our lives because we have reached a place in our journey where we know that we will never be able to find sustainable refreshment in any rest that we can provide ourselves. It's so significant for us to find ways to practice self-care and rest, but we know that's not going to cut it long-term. We need God, in his power, to replenish the deep fatigue that we experience in our lives. Our souls find true rest when we believe and receive the love of Jesus, and we continue to find refreshment as we set aside time to remember the Sabbath. His holiness reminds us who we are and who he is.

———————————

How well do you let God take care of you?

———————————

# DAY 24

---

# ONE ANOTHER

A new commandment I give to you, that you love
one another: just as I have loved you, you also are
to love one another. By this all people will know that
you are my disciples, if you have love for one another.

JOHN 13:34-35

When we dedicate ourselves toward praying with and for
others, it breeds a profound sense of unity. We develop a
desire to be together and to serve each other well. It calibrates
our focus as people on mission in the way of Jesus. Praying
for and serving others helps to produce rest in our lives, as
it moves our direct focus off ourselves and onto the needs of
those around us. We find rest when we take steps to remember the world doesn't revolve around us.

In John 13:34–35, Jesus says that his followers should model their love for each other after his example. He assures them that the way they love one another will let people know the legitimacy of their faith. I've heard it said at times that Christians are better known for what they are against than whom they live for. This is a sad but all-too-often true commentary. What if our lives were marked by the true devotion we have for our savior, and the desire to see his love lived out in the world every day? These are some of the ways the New Testament describes how that would look:

- We are at peace with one another (Mark 9:50).

- We honor and are devoted to one another (Rom 12:10).

- We serve one another (Gal 5:13).

- We carry each other's burdens (Gal 6:2).

- We are patient with one another (Eph 4:2).

- We are kind and compassionate, forgiving one another (Eph 4:32).

- In humility, we consider others better than ourselves (Phil 2:3).

- We do not lie to one another (Col 3:9).

- We build up one another (1 Thess 5:11).

- We make our love increase for one another
  (1 Thess 3:12).

The most vivid example of selfless love is shown when Jesus gets up from the dinner table and washes his disciples' feet. John writes, "When he had washed their feet and put on his outer garments and resumed his place, he said to them, 'Do you understand what I have done to you? You call me Teacher and Lord, and you are right, for so I am. If I then, your Lord and Teacher, have washed your feet, you also ought to wash one another's feet. For I have given you an example, that you also should do just as I have done to you" (John 13:12–15).

As followers of Jesus, we desire to serve one another in this way.

---

What are some ways that you can grow in
your practice of the "one another" verses?

# WHERE ARE YOU PLANTED?

If we live by the Spirit,
let us also keep in step with the Spirit.

GALATIANS 5:25

My wife had always wanted to plant a garden. One day, she went to the garden supply store to pick out some plants she thought would look pretty in the backyard. She worked hard to plant her choices properly and care for them well. She watered them regularly. But, after about a week and a half, one set of plants just seemed to be dying. My wife was concerned that maybe she had purchased some plants that were already dead and, not wanting to waste money, returned to the store to ask why they weren't growing. "Where did you plant them?" the associate immediately asked. My wife went on to describe where and how she planted them. "Oh," said the associate, "that's your problem right there. There is nothing wrong with the plants; they just won't grow where you planted them. Try moving them to the other side of the garden." Sure enough, when my wife moved them, they began to thrive.

Too often, I've chosen the path that I think is best, the plan that I desire, and the method I think will fulfill it. I would end up planting myself where *I* think I need to be, rather than asking God where I need to be planted in order to flourish.

I think of an instance early in the Bible when God told a man named Abram where he wanted him to be. "Go to a place that I will show you," was the direction administered by God. You might wonder, "Where was the place?" Abram didn't know either, but he trusted that God would show him. The only way he would know he'd arrived is if he remained ready to listen.

Rather than choosing our own path and following our own impulses alone, we need to learn to "keep in step with the Spirit," who can lead and guide us in ways that will keep us in rhythm with God. Living life as a continual guessing game based on our own best ideas can produce anxiety, stress, and worry. We need to allow God to lead us to where we should plant our roots.

How can you grow in the ways you keep
in step with the Spirit?

DAY 26

_____

# A HIDDEN LIFE WITH GOD

Blessed are the pure in heart, for they shall see God.

MATTHEW 5:8

If our lives are filled with constant movement and busyness, we won't have a proper understanding of the condition of our inner world. We will focus solely on the maintenance of what is seen by others, managing the perceptions of our spirituality rather than its true legitimacy. It's kind of like only caring about the cosmetic appearance of a car and forgetting to see if the engine works properly to make the car go. I love how *The Message* version of Matthew 5:8 reads. It says, "You're blessed when you get your inside world—your mind and heart—put right. Then you can see God in the outside world."

Henri Nouwen writes, "If we don't have a hidden life with God, our public life for God cannot bear fruit."[9] When we finally surrender to the idea that the gospel and rest inform every aspect of our lives, we begin to work and live from a genuine and sustainable place. Our hearts become a reflection of the heart of God as we live life on earth. It is important for us to note that we can say and do all the right things and not be experiencing the connectedness and overflow that comes from an intimate relationship with Christ. "For out of the abundance of the heart his mouth speaks" (Prov 4:23; Luke 6:45). When prayer becomes a focus and practice in our ministry, powerful things can begin to happen.

Eugene Peterson writes, "Prayer ... is the means by which we get everything in our lives out in the open before God."[10] Prayer is a rhythm that requires us to be vulnerable before the Lord, and in that context we can explore our heart's true intentions and motivations. We know that the Lord knows our hearts and has the power to answer and speak to us. If this weren't true, we wouldn't pray to him. Because we know of his great power, we do not puff our chests in pride before him, but we realize who we are in light of his presence, which helps us to gain perspective in every aspect of our worldview (Ps 131). This type of vulnerability and connection with God allows us to live from a genuine and fruitful place.

---

How is your hidden life with God?

---

DAY 27

---

# LIFE SHAPES
# OUR THEOLOGY

Rather, speaking the truth in love,
we are to grow up in every way into him
who is the head, into Christ.

EPHESIANS 4:15

Growing up on the East Coast, from time to time we'd travel out to the Jersey Shore. One thing I loved to do at the beach was look for sea glass. Now, this may not seem like a fun thing to collect, but sea glass is beautiful. Because these broken pieces of glass tumble back and forth in the saltwater and along the sand for extended periods of time, they end up with smooth edges and unique textures. No single piece of sea glass is what it used to be.

We all have thoughts and ideas about God and the world. This belief system is called our theology. As we move through life, and different circumstances become a part of our internal conversation over years and time, our theology intersects with reality. The ebbs and flows of life begin to shape our beliefs. Just like sea glass, the essence of our faith doesn't change, but the implementation of these thoughts in life conversation helps to smooth some of the sharp edges and provide interesting texture.

As followers of Jesus, we want to celebrate the essential beliefs that unify us in faith in Christ. We believe that the power of the Holy Spirit and Christ's love is what compels and moves us. As we hold fast to our beliefs, we want to be aware of the way we communicate and live them out amongst one another. If we aren't careful, the sharp edges of how we live out our theology can cut others as we interact with them. There are, indeed, hard truths that we learn from Scripture and from following the way of the kingdom. But if we understand how life shapes our theology, we will begin to see the beauty in one another's story and become gracious in how we speak to each other. When Ephesians says that "we are to grow up in every way into him who is the head, into Christ," it means a process of continual maturity and formation as we fix our eyes on God.

———————————

Are there any "sharp edges" in your life that keep you
from interacting with others graciously?

———————————

---

# YOUR PEOPLE

And let us consider how to stir up one another
to love and good works, not neglecting to meet
together, as is the habit of some, but encouraging
one another, and all the more as you see
the Day drawing near.

HEBREWS 10:24-25

Over time, I've learned that it is really important for us to find "our people." These are the folks with whom we will share the joys and pains of life with us as we journey forward. "Our people" will not only provide comfort and care for us and our families, but they will also help us to become the men and women God wants us to be. Living as this type of friend might look like sharing a hard truth in order to point your friend to freedom. Other times this might simply look like sitting with someone in their pain as they process.

Timothy Keller says, "Our character is mainly shaped by our primary social community—the people with whom we eat, play, converse, counsel, and study."[11] We should all look at our current relationships and see how this is true. It is vital for us to find people who are willing to journey with us toward Christ with vulnerability and transparency. If we operate solely in a mode of isolation, we are restricting ourselves from experiencing the benefits associated with genuine connection. As it says in Hebrews, "Let us consider how to stir up one another to love and good works, not neglecting to meet together, as is the habit of some, but encouraging one another, and all the more as you see the Day drawing near."

Our lives are enriched by the goodness of being in a relationship with others. C. S. Lewis once said, "Friendship is the greatest of worldly goods. Certainly to me it is the chief happiness of life. If I had to give a piece of advice to a young man about a place to live, I think I should say, 'Sacrifice almost everything to live where you can be near your friends.' "[12] He believed friendship was essential.

For some, these words shine a light on a deficiency of these types of relationships and can make us feel sad. This is understandable, and it emphasizes the importance of both praying for these types of connections and positioning ourselves to be open to new relationships. I take great comfort in knowing that God is near to the brokenhearted (Ps 34:18).

Through transition, difficulty, pain, and joy, I have been fortunate to have friends who have loved me well. We all have great cause to be thankful for the folks God has placed in our lives who have invested in, challenged, encouraged, and loved us well. I hope we continue to move beyond contentment with "surface" relationships and desire to connect with one another deeply. Understanding that we are not alone in the community of the kingdom of God produces a sense of rest.

———————————

Who are "your people"?

_____

# LIGHTNING AND THUNDER

And the angel said to them, "Fear not, for behold,
I bring you good news of great joy that
will be for all the people."

LUKE 2:10

Since moving to the Nashville area, I have experienced some pretty wild thunderstorms. The flashes of lightning can be both beautiful and frightening. The thunder can be so intense and loud that it will shake our house. There are a couple of things I remember learning about lightning and thunder in my childhood science classes. When lightening breaks into the atmosphere, the resulting noise we hear is thunder. I also remember learning that the closer you are to the lightning, the more quickly you hear the thunder. This illustration makes me think of what it means to experience joy in our lives.

For a long time, I had a hard time finding joy in my life. I would hear people talk about the Christian life being filled with joy and think, "Maybe I'm missing something, because I don't feel it." I've since realized that I had been looking for joy in the wrong places.

I was attempting to find joy in and of itself, but the truth is that joy is a byproduct of something (or someone) else. In Matthew 13:44, Jesus shares a parable that speaks to this idea. He says, "The kingdom of heaven is like treasure hidden in a field, which a man found and covered up. Then in his joy he goes and sells all that he has and buys that field." In the story, a man discovers the treasure, and his immediate response is joy.

A clearer explanation comes from a verse about some shepherds that we read often during Christmastime. Luke 2:9–11 says, "An angel of the Lord appeared to them, and the glory of the Lord shone around them, and they were filled with great fear. And the angel said to them, 'Fear not, for behold, I bring you good news of great joy that will be for all the people. For unto you is born this day in the city of David a Savior, who is Christ the Lord.' " Joy comes from Jesus! It's like lightning and thunder. When lightning breaks into our atmosphere, thunder is the result. When Jesus breaks in, joy abounds.

Many of us have been looking for our circumstances or situations to bring us joy. When we do this, we end up disappointed, because circumstances can really only determine our happiness or sadness. Joy, true Spirit-led joy, remains in the midst of all circumstances. We will only find true joy when we find Christ.

_____

What has your experience with joy looked like in your life?

---

# TRUST FALL

Go therefore and make disciples of all nations,
baptizing them in the name of the Father and of
the Son and of the Holy Spirit, teaching them to
observe all that I have commanded you.
And behold, I am with you always,
to the end of the age.

MATTHEW 28:19-20

Have you ever experienced a trust fall? I'm talking about the feeling of standing on a platform a few feet off the ground with your back to a group of people with their arms out ready to catch you. Then, with complete faith, you allow yourself to fall back and land in the arms of those waiting. A trust fall is a tangible way to experience faith and trust in fellow humans. The people with their arms outstretched are telling you that you'll be okay, there's nothing to worry about, and they'll catch you—you'll find out soon enough!

Walking out the Christian life on earth is like experiencing a trust fall. The journey we are taking into the future as followers of Jesus is not without mystery. We believe the unseen Spirit of God is leading us. We are leaning back with the assurance that he can hold us and sustain us as we seek to advance the kingdom of God on earth.

It's an exhilarating feeling to let go of all that we know to be comfortable and "normal" and allow ourselves to blindly fall into what we believe to be the call of the Lord on our lives for this season. The assurance we receive through his word has continually proven itself to be true, not only in our own lives but throughout history. We hold firm to the knowledge that he knows what is best for us and will catch us at the end of our trust fall.

Just like falling from the platform, though, there are a few questions that arise right before you allow yourself to lean back and trust Jesus. Am I doing the right thing? Am I going to land safely? Can I trust the promise of being caught? These are all completely reasonable questions. There is a certain amount of assuredness that can only be found once you make it through safely. Until then, we trust in his promises, the assuredness of his words. In Matthew 28, when Jesus' followers are about to step out in faith, Jesus says to them, "I am with you always, to the end of the age" (v. 20).

We have no need to panic during our trust fall. We don't know how the journey will unfold, but we will find rest in the strong arms of Christ.

———————————

What are some ways you may not be trusting God as you step forward in faith?

DAY 31

_____

# GRAND SILENCE

For God alone my soul waits in silence;
from him comes my salvation.

PSALM 62:1

I once spent a weekend in a beautiful monastery in California. As amazing as the fellowship, the grounds, and the incredible hospitality of the residents were, the most impactful thing I experienced was something called the grand silence. From 10 p.m. to 8 a.m., no one would speak. It was an intentional step into a posture of listening and reflection. Even though this seemed like a short period and an easy exercise, it was a bit more challenging than I'd expected.

Obviously, when I was alone, it wasn't too difficult. But the next morning at breakfast, the exercise was a bit more challenging. We all served ourselves a plate of food and sat together at round tables. You heard forks clinking on plates, an occasional sniff or cough, but no one was speaking. You had to embrace the awkward. At 8:01 a.m., there was a sense of relief that you could finally speak, but the result was an increased appreciation for the communication that we had begun to take for granted.

Psalm 141:3 says, "Set a guard, O LORD, over my mouth; keep watch over the door of my lips!" We need to be aware of the things we say and the power of our words, because communication is abundant in our lives. More importantly, dedicating ourselves to times of intentional silence can help us to remember that we need the wisdom that comes from the Spirit, not just from our best thinking.

When I got home from the monastery, one area where I began to institute a "grand silence" was in technology. I selected a definitive start and end time and decided to not engage with any incoming or outgoing messages or information (news, social media, etc.) in that time. I found that setting the start time for the silence motivated me to finish any necessary communication with intention and allowed my mind to rest from the optional outlets that can easily overtake my time for hours. Setting the end time allowed me to start my day without the influence of outside voices and noise that can establish a trajectory for the direction of my thoughts. Rather than let the headlines from the news, messages from others, or the comparison on social media determine my mindset for the day, I make an intentional choice about what I let in, something that will help me interact well with all of those things that will be there, regardless. As you're seeking to establish new rhythms, this may be a way to create some space to rest your mind and also build in some time for the input that you would hope to shape your thinking. Some of us are uncomfortable in silence, and this will help us grow comfortable quieting ourselves in order to hear from God. Practicing this grand silence also reveals to us how often our instincts take us to our phone or other outlets when we start to feel bored or unsettled. When we realize this dependence, it helps us to lean into discovering a remedy.

---

Do you make space for silence? If not, how can you start?

---

# COMPLETE, LACKING IN NOTHING

Not only that, but we rejoice in our sufferings,
knowing that suffering produces endurance,
and endurance produces character,
and character produces hope,
and hope does not put us to shame,
because God's love has been poured
into our hearts through the Holy Spirit
who has been given to us.

ROMANS 5:3-5

I've heard it said that your deepest wound can be the path to your deepest sense of meaning. Although we don't enjoy or welcome hard times, and it's extremely difficult to see the positives within them, we are promised by God that our trials are not without purpose. The Scriptures tell us that without our trials, we cannot become the man or woman that God intends for us to be, for his glory. Your life tells a story. The twists and turns and highs and lows that you experience become testaments to God's faithfulness as well as encouragement to others. Paul unfolds the progression of how our difficult circumstances help to shape us as we move forward.

First, suffering produces endurance. Paul says that when you suffer, it helps you to learn how to suffer better. Take running, for example. When someone runs for exercise—especially when training for long distances—they run (suffer) so that they can build the endurance to run longer (suffer better). Our difficult experiences strengthen us to endure upcoming trials.

Next, endurance produces character. Our ability to "suffer better" when faced with hard times shapes our character in tangible ways. Think about the people you know who have endured great tragedy or difficulty. We want to hear their stories and learn from their experiences. Some of the greatest art and literature have been products of an individual or group's ability to endure suffering.

Finally, character produces hope. When we see how character is shaped while enduring difficulties, it lets us know that God is redeeming our trials and using them for his glory. Our suffering wasn't purposeless. Hope is produced because we look back on what was desolate and difficult and see how he makes something beautiful in our lives out of the shards of our brokenness. We will never be let down by this hope because we have the presence of the Holy Spirit in our lives, who is our assurance.

Charles Dickens once wrote, "Suffering has been stronger than all other teaching. ... I have been bent and broken, but, I hope, into a better shape."[13] We can find rest in the knowledge that our suffering helps us to become complete, formed into versions of ourselves we could never have otherwise been.

———————

How have you found hope and redemption in
your suffering and hard seasons of life?

---

# CAN/SHOULD

I therefore, a prisoner for the Lord, urge you to walk
in a manner worthy of the calling to which you have
been called, with all humility and gentleness, with
patience, bearing with one another in love, eager to
maintain the unity of the Spirit in the bond of peace.

EPHESIANS 4:1-3

When we are trying to discern whether to do something, we
usually come to a quick conclusion by asking, "*Can* I do it?"
Most times, the answer is yes. We have the ability, strength,
drive, and know-how to do a lot of different things that are
asked of us. And with abundant access to information in our
current day and age, if we don't know how to do something,
we can quickly figure it out. But the "can" question is not
enough to help us live in a way that intentionally minimizes

anxiety, stress, and worry. "Should I do it?" becomes a great filter in our lives.

This is an issue of stewardship. If I asked a financial advisor friend to look after the last bit of money to my name, he would not take that assignment lightly. First of all, his job is to be successful at managing money, so if he did a terrible job with it, a bad reputation could harm his future. Also, knowing the weight and implications of me losing my last bit of money would heighten his sense of accountability and ownership of what happened to it. He would take great pains to pay attention not only to how to protect the money from being lost, but also how to invest it for the greatest gains.

This is how God wants us to view our lives. As we find rest for our souls, we become ambassadors for the message of Jesus. The Bible tells us that we were "bought with a price" by Christ's death, burial, and resurrection (1 Cor 6:20), so our lives are no longer ours to do with what we please, but God's to do what pleases him. As fully submitted followers of Christ, we want to do what he wants us to do. The Bible teaches that though we can do something, it is not always beneficial (1 Cor 6:12). We are living and working from rest when we know that our steps follow God's clear "should" rather than our own impulses.

How will the can/should way of thinking affect
your decision-making process?

---

# REFRESHING

Repent therefore, and turn back, that your sins
may be blotted out, that times of refreshing may
come from the presence of the Lord, and that he
may send the Christ appointed for you, Jesus,
whom heaven must receive until the time for
restoring all the things about which
God spoke by the mouth of
his holy prophets long ago.

ACTS 3:19-21

When I was growing up in New Jersey, in the heat of the
summer, every once in a while someone would take a wrench
to a fire hydrant and cause water to come spraying out. All the
kids in the neighborhood would run home, put on shorts or
a bathing suit, and come back to splash around. When it was
90-plus degrees in mainly concrete and asphalt surroundings,

that first splash of water was both shockingly cold and beautifully soothing. Although the water would feel like it was freezing, you wouldn't dream of moving out of the way, because it was just what you needed to cool you off. Once you got used to the feel of the water, you could run free and play.

There's a story in the book of Acts where Peter and John heal a lame beggar. When Peter sees that the people watching were astonished, he tells them that they shouldn't be, because they healed the man in the name of Jesus. He tells the people that they've been putting their hope in the powers of this world, but now they've clearly seen the power of the living God at work. He goes on to tell them that they need to repent and "turn back" so their sins might be forgiven, and that "times of refreshing" would come from the presence of the Lord.

When the people hear this call to repentance, it has to be shocking, at first. They are simply following the way of the established leadership that had always been there. They are trusting everything that was told to them about Jesus, without question. But they are wrong. They were told that Jesus was dead, but he is alive. They were told he was just a man, but he is God. Similar to the cold water shooting out of that fire hydrant, Peter's words got their attention, and it was going to take a bit to adjust. But once the shock wears off, they realize there is hope and forgiveness. Once they turn to Jesus, they will experience the refreshment they long for. That refreshment comes from the presence of God.

Even today, there are times when we allow ourselves to put our hope and trust in the powers that exist in this world. Whether it's money, power, position, influence, or relationships, if we're not careful we can trust in them more than we trust in Christ. But we are full of hope, because if we repent, turn back, and trust that Jesus' power is above all things, we'll find refreshment and rest in him.

———————————

What does it look like to experience the times of refreshment that come from the presence of the Lord?

DAY 35

---

# LIVING HOPE

Blessed be the God and Father of our
Lord Jesus Christ! According to his great mercy,
he has caused us to be born again to a living hope
through the resurrection of Jesus Christ
from the dead.

1 PETER 1:3

Once, when I was walking through a difficult season, I had
a phone conversation with a friend. He asked me how I
was doing in the wake of losses we experienced and the all-
around hard nature of our current season. Somewhere in
the middle of all of my rambling and attempting to convince
him that I was doing great and that everything was going to
work out fine, he interrupted and said, "Hey, can I say something?" I was a bit thrown off, because I was in the midst of
my hyper-positive monologue when he spoke up.

"Sure," I said, "what's up?" He said, "I want you to know, it's okay not to be okay." This sentence stopped me dead in my tracks. Quite frankly, I had heard and most likely said these very words before. But something about hearing this direct statement from a friend struck a chord deep within me. Oh, how I longed and wanted it to be true, and I had no words in response. In recognition of my silence, he said, "I know it's hard for you to believe, but it's true." There was such a weight off, knowing that I could bring my full self before God and not have to keep up pretenses that everything was fine when my heart was hurting badly.

As helpful as that reminder was from my friend, there was a follow-up idea that deepened my contentment and awareness that God was with me in my pain. I felt like God was saying, "Yes, it's okay to not be okay ... and whether you believe it or not right now, there is a living hope in Jesus Christ." I know myself, and I know there's a possibility that I could become comfortable and content in my "not-okay-ness" and accept this as my reality indefinitely. It's important that we admit when we are out of sorts and don't try to fake our way through our pain. But we shouldn't want to stay there. Our hope is that God meets us in our pain and leads us out into freedom.

What does it mean to you that we have
a living hope in Jesus?

# DAY 36

---

# RESTING ISN'T LAZY

And he said to them, "Come away by
yourselves to a desolate place and rest a while."
For many were coming and going, and
they had no leisure even to eat.

MARK 6:31

As a result of many conversations, I've discovered that some people don't practice a regular rhythm of stopping and resting because they think that it is a sign of weakness. Others have shared with me that they think that if you rest, it is a sign of failure. Let me be absolutely clear about one thing: rest does not automatically equal laziness.

The hope of finding soul rest doesn't mean that we are seeking to establish a life devoid of work. On the contrary, we are hoping to establish a sustainable rhythm that helps us to work from rest. We need the restoration that comes from

God, and in order to receive it, we have to stop. When we are unable to rest, it's like we are saying to God that he can't do his work without our help. Our view of our self-importance, even for the work of the kingdom of God, has caused us to be out of alignment with God's intention for humanity.

Some of us believe that our passion for Jesus justifies never taking time to Sabbath. We love what we do, so we think there is no reason to rest. But let's say someone had to have an extremely long, intense, and intricate surgery. Do you think it would be acceptable for the surgeon to say, "I'm bleary-eyed, haven't slept in a couple of days, and I feel exhausted, but I love what I do, so there is no need for me to take a break"? Of course not. You would protest and say he needs to rest up before he attempts to do something with life-or-death implications. This is an example of how finding rest is—rather than being a marker of weakness or failure—evidence of strength and maturity. We do better work, and make better choices, when we are rested. This is true both physically and spiritually.

It is no secret that we don't know how to rest as a culture. There is something engrained in our DNA that tells us we need to be working to be valued. The drive to work is placed in us by God himself. From our creation, he indeed intended that we would work. But along the way, we became distracted and disconnected from the actual purpose and intent of our work. We began to attach our value, worth, and identity to the work we do. When we rest, we are not being lazy; we are stopping the work of our hands so that we can receive the refreshment that only comes from God's hands.

———————————

Do you have a hard time stopping and resting? What is a step you can take toward developing a rhythm of rest?

DAY 37

# OPEN YOUR HANDS

I stretch out my hands to you;
my soul thirsts for you like a parched land.

PSALM 143:6

Engagement with God's presence isn't instinctual for most
of us. Constant movement and our continual desire to fulfill
our own comfort and satisfaction is more likely the human
impulse that leads us. In the midst of a busy and chaotic life,
we need to be intentional about connecting with our Creator.
When we do this, we increase the space that can be filled with
his goodness, mercy, and rest.

A lot of times, our words communicate that we desire to
connect with God more consistently and on a deeper level,
but our actions and posture say otherwise. It's kind of like
a child, after requesting a piece of candy, was offered it but

then kept her hand closed rather than open to receive it. She has expressed her desire to have it, but she won't take it. We need to posture ourselves to be ready to receive the rest that the Lord desires for us to have.

It is not wise to believe that the only way we can experience the presence of God is if we attend a meeting at a building or attend a church program. Of course, the presence of God can be found in those places, but practicing a rhythm of Sabbath reminds us that God is far greater and bigger than we could ever hope to imagine. Eugene Peterson once wrote, "Sabbath is the time set aside to do nothing so that we can receive everything."[14] The source of the rest that comes from Sabbath transcends the places or events that we attend. The rest we find in God does not originate in this world, and we should be thankful for this, because that means it is not limited by the bounds of what we know and understand.

---

How can you posture your life to receive
the rest God desires for you?

# DAY 38

---

# LIVING SACRIFICE

I appeal to you therefore, brothers, by the mercies of
God, to present your bodies as a living sacrifice,
holy and acceptable to God, which is
your spiritual worship.

ROMANS 12:1

As followers of Jesus, the best thing we can celebrate together is the beauty of the great love and grace that Christ has shown us. Because of his great mercies, our proper response is to be what Paul calls a "living sacrifice" in Romans 12:1.

The words "living sacrifice" together don't make much sense at first. It's actually an oxymoron. But reading Paul's words in Romans just before this verse, we understand that this isn't the case. We are alive in Christ because we begin to live solely led by his desires and purposes for us. We are also an offering to God because we have chosen to sacrifice our way and plans for the better ones God has for us. Of course, we realize that, because of our flesh, this is a highly tricky prospect. Thankfully, the verse continues to reveal how this can happen: "Do not be conformed to this world, but be transformed by the renewal of your mind, that by testing you may discern what is the will of God, what is good and acceptable and perfect" (Rom 12:2).

Imagine yourself holding a lump of clay. Let's pretend that you were asked to *conform* that lump of clay—say, to the shape of a ball. You would begin to roll the clay around in your hands until it started to make a spherical shape, thus becoming your best representation of a ball. Now, imagine that you were asked to *transform* this clay into an actual baseball. We might be able to manipulate the clay to mimic what a baseball looks like, but to turn it into something that is made from cowhide and thread would be a completely different task. To "conform" the clay would be to make it take the shape of something. To "transform" the clay would be to turn the clay itself into a completely different substance altogether.

We have the power to conform. Only God can transform.

Our goal isn't to take the shape of the world that we see around us but to allow the Lord to redeem and make us new in it. That God has the power to do this is fantastic news. In our humanity, we can attempt to change our behaviors, but this type of effort cannot be sustained. God, on the other hand, graciously restores us from the inside out. He does this by transforming and renewing the very way we think and comprehend reality. The verse goes on to say that when we are transformed, it helps us to discern, or figure out, what the Lord desires for us.

---

What does it look like for you or your family
to exist as "living sacrifices"?

---

# EXTRA BAGGAGE

Therefore, since we are surrounded by so great
a cloud of witnesses, let us also lay aside every weight,
and sin which clings so closely, and let us run with
endurance the race that is set before us.

HEBREWS 12:1

When we were moving from California to Tennessee, we had to move everything we owned across the country in one moving truck. To do this, we had to go through boxes that we hadn't opened for a long time. Anyone who has ever moved knows that this process can produce varying results. Some instances create a level of excitement to discover things you've been missing for a while. More often in our case, though, we'd come across things and wonder, "Why in the world do we still have this?!"

Of course, the best thing to do to avoid this would be to monitor what we are bringing into our home in the first place. Or, we could regularly go through and evaluate what needs to be kept and what doesn't. Purging is hard, though, because you have to make difficult decisions about what to hold onto and what to release. It's much easier to tuck stuff away and deal with it later.

As you have been spending this intentional time connecting with Christ, you may have stumbled upon some practices or rhythms in your life that require a similar decision. It's probably the habits you hold on to that weigh you down or trip you up in life, and you're wondering why you keep them around. We should ask ourselves, "Do I really want to bring this with me?" We are attempting to build a future with a new perspective. Rather than being content with dragging around our old bags and boxes, we have asked the Lord to show us what is keeping us from thriving.

There is a quote by Dietrich Bonhoeffer that goes, "We must be ready to allow ourselves to be interrupted by God."[15] Rather than just continuing with life as usual, we want to find freedom from the baggage that we've been carrying. When we open ourselves to the opportunity to be surprised by the Spirit of God, we find freedom and refreshment in unloading our baggage. As it says in Hebrews, we want to "lay aside every weight, and sin which clings so closely, and let us run with endurance the race that is set before us."

Let's begin a new season with a fresh perspective and a little less baggage.

---

What baggage do you want to leave behind as you move into this new season?

---

# A WORD IN THE
# WILDERNESS

Therefore, behold, I will allure her, and bring her into
the wilderness, and speak tenderly to her.

HOSEA 2:14

When most people refer to being in a "wilderness season," it is usually with negative connotations. The wilderness is a term often used to describe a period of time you would like to escape as soon as possible. We don't know where we are going, what will happen, or how long it will take. If we think we are in the wilderness, we want out.

But, when I was in Israel, I learned that many people in that culture hold a different perspective of the wilderness. They would say you should voluntarily enter the wilderness. They would say that the wilderness is a place of listening and waiting. If you were to ask how they arrived at that perspective, they might reply, "Haven't you read the Bible?"

The Hebrew word *davar* means "word" or "thing." And the term *midbar* means "wilderness." The people of Israel knew that God was known to give a *davar* in the *midbar*, or a word in the wilderness. Moses sees the burning bush and receives a *davar* in the *midbar*. Elisha was sustained by God and received a *davar* in the *midbar*. Jesus, immediately after he is baptized, is led by the Spirit of God into the *midbar*.

Now, having been in the very wilderness that is referenced in the Bible, it is not incorrect to say that the wilderness is uncomfortable. It is! Extreme heat, little to no vegetation, and arduous terrain. But, when it comes to hearing from God, there are some immense benefits. There are no distractions. You would need to be fully dependent on God to sustain you. And, most vivid to me, it is completely silent. If you wanted to go to a place where you could hear God clearly with no distractions or noise, the wilderness was it.

Maybe this idea will help us as we navigate what it means to be a follower of Jesus in our day and age. Maybe we can reframe our perspective of wilderness and begin to intently seek what God is wanting to say to us right now. Rather than focusing all of our attention and energy on figuring out how to get out of the situation we are in, maybe we can begin to say, "What do you want me to learn before I go?" In Israel, one of my teachers told me of a saying common among those who read the Bible through a Middle-Eastern lens: "How do I bring the wilderness with me?"

———————————

How has your perspective of the wilderness changed?

———————————

# NOTES

1    Henri Nouwen quoted in Dallas Willard, "A Cup Running Over," in *The Art and Craft of Biblical Preaching: A Comprehensive Resource for Today's Communicators*, ed. Haddon Robinson and Craig Brian Larson (Grand Rapids: Zondervan, 2009).

2    G. K. Chesterton, *Orthodoxy* (New York: John Lane Company, 1909), 212.

3    John Calvin, *Institutes of the Christian Religion* (Peabody, MA: Hendrickson Publishers Inc., 2007).

4    Ronald Rolheiser, *The Holy Longing: The Search for a Christian Spirituality* (New York: Doubleday, 1999), 3.

5    Dan B. Allender and Tremper Longman III, *The Cry of the Soul* (Dallas: Word, 1994), 24–25. Quoted in Peter Scazzero and Warren Bird, *The Emotionally Healthy Church: A Strategy for Discipleship that Actually Changes Lives* (Grand Rapids: Zondervan, 2003).

6    Frederick Buechner, *Telling Secrets* (New York: HarperOne, 2000).

7    C. J. H. Higgins, *The God I Don't Understand: Reflections on Tough Questions of Faith* (Grand Rapids: Zondervan, 2008).

8    Marva Dawn, *Keeping the Sabbath Wholly: Ceasing, Resting, Embracing, Feasting* (Grand Rapids: Eerdmans, 1989).

9    Henri Nouwen, *Bread for the Journey: A Daybook of Wisdom and Faith* (Grand Rapids: Zondervan, 2006).

10   Eugene Peterson, *The Message* (Colorado Springs: NavPress, 2002).

11   Timothy Keller, *Center Church: Doing Balanced, Gospel-Centered Ministry in Your City* (Grand Rapids: Zondervan, 2012).

12   C. S. Lewis, *The Collected Letters of C. S. Lewis, Volume II: Books, Broadcasts, and the War 1931–1949* (New York: HarperOne, 2004).

13   Charles Dickens, *Great Expectations* (New York: Penguin, 2002).

14   Eugene Peterson, *Tell It Slant: A Conversation on the Language of Jesus in His Stories and Prayers* (Grand Rapids: Eerdmans, 2008), 82.

15   Dietrich Bonhoeffer, *Life Together: The Classic Exploration of Christian Community* (New York: HarperOne, 2009).